# Beckonings

## Gwendolyn Brooks

Broadside Press, 12651 Old Mill   Detroit, Michigan 48238

# TENTH ANNIVERSARY EDITION

This project is supported by a grant from the National Endowment for the Arts in Washington, D.C., a Federal agency.

Cover Art by Raymond Brooks

## ACKNOWLEDGMENTS

*Ebony, Broadside Series, Black Scholar*

ISBN 0-910296-37-5

$3.00

Manufactured in U.S.A.

## RAYMOND MELVIN BROOKS

He found industriousness an engrossing challenge.
He found people experiences in enrichment.
He found everyday living a tasty fruit,
an enjoyable nourishment.
All of his life
people responded, people said "yes!" to
his affectionate, warm and cheerful presence, to
his exuberant charming, to
his involving smile.

He knew how to put paint to paper—
made the paper speak and sing.
But he was chiefly a painter of days and the daily,
with a talent for life color, life pattern:
a talent for jeweling use and the usual,
a talent for practical style.

# CONTENTS

# THE BOY DIED IN MY ALLEY

*to Running Boy*

The Boy died in my alley
without my Having Known.
Policeman said, next morning,
"Apparently died Alone."

"You heard a shot?" Policeman said.
Shots I hear and Shots I hear.
I never see the Dead.

The Shot that killed him yes I heard
as I heard the Thousand shots before;
careening tinnily down the nights
across my years and arteries.

Policeman pounded on my door.
"Who is it?" "POLICE!" Policeman yelled.
"A Boy was dying in your alley.
A Boy is dead, and in your alley.
And have you known this Boy before?"

I have known this Boy before.
I have known this Boy before, who
ornaments my alley.
I never saw his face at all.
I never saw his futurefall.
But I have known this Boy.

I have always heard him deal with death.
I have always heard the shout, the volley.
I have closed my heart-ears late and early.
And I have killed him ever.

I joined the Wild and killed him
with knowledgeable unknowing.
I saw where he was going.
I saw him Crossed. And seeing,
I did not take him down.

He cried not only "Father!"
but "Mother!
Sister!
Brother."
The cry climbed up the alley.
It went up to the wind.
It hung upon the heaven
for a long
stretch-strain of Moment.

The red floor of my alley
is a special speech to me.


FIVE MEN
AGAINST THE THEME
"MY NAME IS RED HOT.
YO NAME AIN DOODLEY SQUAT."

*Hoyt and Lerone, Dudley*
*and Haki and Lu.*

This is the time of the crit, the creeple, and the makeiteer.

Our warfare is through the trite traitors, through
the ice-committees, through
the mirages, through
the suburban petals, through
toss-up, and tin-foil.

Therefore we are thankful for steel.
We
are thanful
for steel.

# TO JOHN OLIVER KILLENS IN 1975

John,
look at our mercy, the massiveness that it is not.
Look at our "unity," look at our
"black solidarity."
Dim, dull and dainty.
Ragged. And we
grow colder; we
grow colder.
See our
tatter-time.

You were a mender.

You were a sealer of tremblings and long trepidations.
And always, with you, the word kindness was not
a jingling thing but an
eye-tenderizer, a
heart-honeyer.

Therefore we turn, John, to you.
Interrupting self-raiding.We pause in our falling.
To ask another question of your daylight.

# STEAM SONG

*Hostilica hears Al Green*

That Song it sing the sweetness
like a good Song can,
and make a woman want to
run out and find her man.

Ain got no pretty mansion.
Ain got no ruby ring.
My man is my only
necessary thing.

That Song boil up my blood
like a good Song can.
It make this woman want to
run out and find her man.

# ELEGY IN A RAINBOW

*Moe Belle's double love song.*

When I was a little girl
  Christmas was exquisite.
  I didn't touch it.
I didn't look at it too closely.
  To do that to do that
might nullify the shine.

Thus with a Love
that has to have a Home
like the Black Nation,
like the Black Nation
defining its own Roof
that no one else can see.

9

# A BLACK WEDDING SONG

*First dedicated to
Charles and La Tanya,
Allen and Glenda,
Haki and Safisha.*

## I

This love is a rich cry over
the deviltries and the death.
A weapon-song. Keep it strong.

Keep it strong.
Keep it logic and Magic and lightning and Muscle.

Strong hand in strong hand, stride to
the Assault that is promised you (knowing
no armor assaults a pudding or a mush.)

Here is your Wedding Day.
Here is your launch.

Come to your Wedding Song.

## II

For you
I wish the kindness that romps or sorrows along.
Or kneels.
I wish you the daily forgiveness of each other.
For war comes in from the World
and puzzles a darling duet—
tangles tongues,
tears hearts, mashes minds;
there will be the need to forgive.

I wish you jewels of black love.

Come to your Wedding Song.

# HORSES GRAZE

Cows graze.
Horses graze.
They
eat
eat
eat.
Their graceful heads
are bowed
bowed
bowed
in majestic oblivion.
They are nobly oblivious
to your follies,
your inflation,
the knocks and nettles of administration.
They
eat
eat
eat.
And at the crest of their brute satisfaction,
with wonderful gentleness, in affirmation,
they lift their clean calm eyes and they lie down
and love the world.
They speak with their companions.
They do not wish that they were otherwhere.
Perhaps they know that creature feet may press
only a few earth inches at a time,
that earth is anywhere earth,
that an eye may see,
wherever it may be,
the Immediate arc, alone, of life, of love.

In Sweden,
China,
Afrika,
in India or Maine
the animals are sane;
they know and know and know
there's ground below
and sky
up high.


## "WHEN HANDED A LEMON, MAKE LEMONADE"

*(title by Anonymous)*

I've lived through lemons,
sugaring them.
"When handed a lemon,
make lemonade."
That is what
some sage has said.
"When handed a lemon,
make lemonade."

There is always a use
for lemon juice.

Do you know what to do with
trouble, children?
Make lemonade. Make lemonade.
"Handed a lemon, make lemonade."

## SAMMY CHESTER LEAVES "GODSPELL" AND VISITS *UPWARD BOUND* ON A LAKE FOREST LAWN, BRINGING WEST AFRIKA.

"WEST SIDE." screamed Sammy Chester.
I was born at 16th and Homan "
          I was BORN born born.
Unhalt hands—
body leantall rocking—
fierce innocent Afrikan rhythm . . .

West side. West AFRIKA.
Bursting back
free of the fibreless fury—
free of the
plastic platitudes—
free of the
strange stress, ordained ordure and high hell.

Afrika laughing through clean teeth,
through open sun, through fruit-flavored music that
applauded out of the other.

Afrika denied
Lake Forest limplush on that sunny afternoon.

# FRIEND

Walking with you
shuts off shivering.
Here we are.
Here we are.
I am with you to share and to bear and to care.
This is warm.
I want you happy, I want you warm.
Your Friend for our forever is what I am.
Your Friend in thorough thankfulness.
It is the evening of our love.
Evening is hale and whole.
Evening shall not go out.
Evening is comforting flame.
Evening is comforting flame.

# BOYS. BLACK.

*a preachment*

Boys. Black. Black Boys.
Be brave to battle for your breath and bread.
Your heads hold clocks that strike the new time of day.
Your hearts are
legislating Summer Weather now.
      Cancel Winter.

Up, boys. Boys black. Black boys.
Invade now where you can or can't prevail.
Take this:
           there's fertile ground beneath the pseudo-ice.
Take this:
           sharpen your hatchets. Force into the green.
Boys, in all your Turnings and your Churnings,
remember Afrika.
Call your singing and your bringing,
your pulse, your ultimate booming in
the not-so-narrow temples of your Power—
call all that, that is your Poem, AFRIKA.
Although you know
so little of that long leaplanguid land,
our tiny union
is the dwarfmagnificent.
Is the busysimple thing.

See, say, salvage.
Legislate.
Enact our inward law.

In the precincts of a nightmare all contrary
be with your sisters hope for our enhancement.
Hurry.
Force through the sludge.
Wild thick scenery subdue.

Because
the eyeless Leaders flutter, tilt, and fail.
The followers falter, peculiar, eyeless too.
Force through the sludge. Force, whether
God is a Thorough and a There,
or a mad child,
playing
with a floorful of toys,
mashing
whatwhen he wills. Force, whether
God is spent pulse, capricious, or a yet-to-come.

And boys,
young brothers, young brothers—
beware the imitation coronations.
Beware
the courteous paper of kingly compliments.

Beware
the easy griefs.
It is too easy to cry "ATTICA "
and shock thy street,
and purse thy mouth,
and go home to thy "Gunsmoke." Boys,
black boys,
beware the easy griefs
that fool and fuel nothing.

I tell you
I love You
and I trust You.
Take my Faith.
Make of my Faith an engine.
Make of my Faith
a Black Star. I am Beckoning.